Great Quotes

by Gary Vardon.

Introduction

You will be exposed to the wisdom of the ages in this book. You will be inspired, informed, and entertained. You will have information that you can use in your own life. So, be prepared to learn. I will give you a number of quotes from great men. Some of these I will not comment on further and I will go onto other great quotes. Others merit comment.

The wisdom of the ages does not go out of fashion. One advantage of writing a book like this is that it will stay current. Technology changes advances rendering much old technology obsolete. Wisdom remains. Truth does not die.

Shakespeare said, "Men of a few words are the best man." By writing a number of books including *Consulting for Profit, Jokes?* and *Do It Right* as well as *Great Quotes* I lost that distinction. These books are available from PublishAmerica and can be purchased from Amazon and read on a Kindle.

Enjoy.

Main Body

My first quote is, "I quote others only the better to express myself," and that's by Montague. That's what I'm doing in this book. The second quote is, "The wisdom of the wise and the experience of ages may be preserved by quotation." Again I'm doing that. I'm not unique. This is hardly the most comprehensive work but the quotes are powerful you can benefit by listening to these quotes. "There is nothing so ridiculous that has not at some time been said by some philosopher." And I think that is a danger that you may face in other collections of quotations, in that people will expose you to quotations and people quoted may be saying things that are erroneous and ridiculous. And we try to shield the reader from that, at least to a certain extent. So these are not just a random collection of quotations. But these are quotations that we feel, for the most part, are quite correct and useful. And in the few cases they're not necessarily totally correct, but they're quite inspiring, so I'll give you those types of quotations also. In the very few cases, we'll give you ideas that we feel are wrong and will comment on why they're wrong. That is not going to happen too often.

"There are more things in Heaven and Earth, Horatio, that are not dreamt of in your philosophy," and that's from Shakespeare. And that's very true. Hopefully you'll find that out here in this book. "Will this be madness if there is method in it?" That's from Shakespeare. I hope you don't consider this tape to be madness, but I do hope you find some method in it. "If you have knowledge, let others light their candles by it." That's what we're doing here. We're letting others light their candle by our knowledge. "If a little knowledge is dangerous, where is the man who has so much to be out of danger?" That's from Thomas Henry Huxley. Hopefully after listening to this tape, you'll be a little closer to being out of danger. Obviously this quote builds on another quote that is well-known. The quote being, "A little knowledge is a dangerous thing."

This is definitely true in some fields more than others. For example rock climbing is a highly dangerous activity that one should not enter into without knowing your knots, repelling and belaying techniques. Skilled fellow climbers and a good guidebook are also necessities as is quality equipment including your rope. Your life is hanging on the end of that rope.

Other fields such as photography are a lot more forgiving. The worst that could happen to you with photography is wasting film. In this digital age you can just hit the delete button and nothing is wasted. Plus you can learn from your mistakes.

"Common sense is the knack of seeing things as they are and doing things as they ought to be done." Easier said than done. This may be true for a lot of wisdom. Pointing to the right thing to do is sometimes easy. Doing it is frequently not. For example a salesman could be told to make a lot of sales calls to get more sales. But this takes time and effort and knowing people so it's easier said than done. Socrates said, "There are only one good, namely, knowledge, and only one evil, namely, ignorance. And hopefully this book will help combat ignorance and spread knowledge. Disraeli said, "Ignorance never settles a question." Edwards said, "Great objects from great minds."

"Against stupidity, the very gods contend in vain." That's from Schiller. And they don't appear to be winning. Hopefully you won't find much stupidity in this book. "The more we study, the more we discover our ignorance." That's from Shelley. That's one of the purposes of study namely to point out where one is ignorant and where one has fallacies. Unfortunately, some people have a lot of vested interest in their accumulated theories and stores of information and so are not open to new ideas and new ways of structuring reality.

"He who loses hope may then part with anything." That's from Congreve. Hopefully you won't lose hope. "No legacy is as rich as honesty." That's from Shakespeare. "Difficulties are things that show what men are." Overcoming difficulties is one of the keys to success. This is especially true in business where difficulties abound. One of the marks of the successful business man is the ability to overcome obstacles such as lack of regulatory approval, sagging demand for a product, loss of key employees, being sued, lack of time, unfavorable publicity, heavy expenses and shifting markets.

"God heals and the doctor takes the fee. " That's from Franklin. A fundamental criticism of the medical profession is just that people will heal spontaneously and the doctor and medical system get paid for that. "Sow an act and you'll reap a habit; sow a habit and you'll reap a character; sow a character and reap a destiny." And that's from G. D. Boardman. Good habits are a key to success. This is another example of advice it's easy to give and correct but more difficult to implement. Of course what a good habit is and what a good character is a somewhat debatable. There are some things that most do agree on. Being a hard worker, being consistent in providing quality, avoiding addictive drugs, getting exercise and being honest are some examples.

"Most unhappy of all men is he who believes himself to be so," and that's from Hume. Abraham Lincoln said something to the effect that you're only as happy as you think you are. Very true. Reframing can lift your mood. Being happy is not hard. Just think that things are the way they should be and you will be happy. Just focus on the moment and you be happy.

"Him who had moved the world first moved himself," and that's from Socrates. And that quote bears commenting on. I think it verges on something which could be called sophistical; in other words, something that sounds very profound but really doesn't mean too much. At least it can be interpreted that way as something as sophistical, but I think it could also mean that you should improve yourself before you go out and try to improve institutions or other people or before you try to do great deeds. In that sense, it may be quite profound and quite true. But like some of the other quotes here, it could be considered to be somewhat sophistical in the sense that it's appearing very deep, but in reality, not saying anything. Cicero said that, "All great men are, in some degree, inspired." Of course, one would ask how he defines a great man and how he would define being inspired, but there's probably some truth to that. In other words, they're probably enthusiastic about something. Of course, you would say that if somebody weren't inspired, he wasn't too great, and so on. So that, again, that's somewhat of a nebulous thing to say, but it may well be quite true, though.

No work of quotations would be complete without quoting the great Nietzsche, and so I'll quote Nietzsche. "Weakness is the greatest of crime." "The over-civilized man, who has lost the great fighting, masterful virtues -- in him there is abomination." That's from Nietzsche, too. "Thank God for the iron in the blood of our fathers!" That's from Nietzsche. "What is good? ye ask. To be brave is good. Thus live your life of obedience and war." "Man is something to be surpassed." "I do not advise you to conclude peace, but to conquer" More Nietzsche. "Thus would I have man and woman. Fit for warfare, the one; fit for giving birth, the other." "When men fear righteous war when women fear motherhood, well, it is that they should vanish from the earth." "A nation that has trained itself to a career of unwarlike and isolated ease is bound in the end to go down before other nations which have not lost the manly and adventurous qualities." More Nietzsche: "Sympathy is both the multiplier of misery and the conserver of misery." Tanner said in the same line as Nietzsche, "Those who minister to poverty and disease are accomplices to the two worst of all crimes." I'm not saying that I necessarily agree with everything that Nietzsche said, but I do think they give us pause to think. Our society may well overemphasize pacifistic virtues and misguided altruism and underestimate training for warfare and self-defense.

Viscount Morley of Blackburn said, "it is not enough to do good, one must do it right way." He said further, "No man can climb out of the limitations of his own character."

Nietzsche said when talking about the Superman, "You I advise not to work but to fight." This quote brought tears to my eyes when I first heard it. This is a refreshing change from the usual pacifist malarkey that one hears bandied about.

He said further, "Man is a bridge between the ape and the Superman."

Gen. MacArthur said, "the cause of war is undefended wealth." The United States in 2011 spends about a nickel per dollar of GNP on the military. That's a small price to pay to protect the other 95%. The United States should not worry about spending too much on national defense. We should be concerned about an inadequate military to protect our nation and our allies.

Peace through strength is the motto of the National Defense industrial Association.

A quote that's original to yours truly is study war, study war never don't study war.

I'd like to quote Theodore Roosevelt in his talking about the strenuous life. "I wish to preach," it begins, "not the doctrine of ignoble ease, but the doctrine of the strenuous life, the life of toil and effort of labor and strife; to preach the highest form of success which comes not to the man who desires mere easy peace, but to the man who does not shrink from danger, from hardship, or from bitter toil; and from who, out of these, wins the splendid ultimate triumph.

Francis Galton said, "The instincts and facilities of different men and races differ in a variety of ways almost as profoundly as those of animals in different cages of a zoological gardens."

Only fools ignore racial differences.

 William Makepeace Thackery said, "Nothing like bloods are in horses, dogs, and men." George Elliot said, "Greed is stronger than pasture." "Cannot hate; cannot love." Swinburne said that.

"It is a silly goose that goes to a fox's sermon." H. D. Baun said that in his *Handbook of Proverbs.* I hope none of you out there are like silly gooses. "Facts are stubborn things, they are." Lesage said that, and I think that's one of the key concepts of science. Scientists do not invent facts and they do not ignore them. "To be healthful is to be fruitful, and fruitfulness is political power." Oswald Spengler said that. "Without isolation or the prevention of intercrossing organic evolution is in no place possible." G. J. Romanes said that. Julian Huxley had a very profound thought: "Evolution is the most powerful and the most comprehensive idea that has ever arisen on Earth."

"Evolution is the keyword which will either answer all the riddles which surround us or put us on the way to their solution." And that's by Ernst Haeckel. I tend to agree with that. I've studied biology enough to recognize the profound importance of evolution in biology. Another quote from Nietzsche: "He who cannot obey himself is commanded." Plato said, "We are bound to our bodies like an oyster to its shell."

Oswald Spengler said, "To separate soul and body is to have neither." Very profound.

And then on the other hand Gandhi said, "The body is only a prison," but if you had a body like Gandhi, you'd say the same thing yourself. The body despisers are themselves to be despised "Though it be disfigured by many defects, to whom is his own body not dear?" Okay, I'll give you another shot of Nietzsche: "Everything ugly weakens and depresses man; reminds him of decay, danger, and impotence. " Ladybird Johnson said, "Ugliness creates bitterness. Ugliness is an eroding force on the people of our land." "The first and the last thing which is required of genius is a love of truth." Goethe said that. It's true. Richter said, "Weaklings have to lie."

Ralph Waldo Emerson said, "A nation never falls but by suicide." An English proverb goes, "It's an ill bird that fouls its own nest." I think that should encourage us to be more environmentally conscious and try to preserve the environment better. "There are two things necessary for the continued existence of a race: It must remain itself and it must breed its best." Lothrop Stoddard said that. "No man can answer for his own valor or courage till he has been in danger." "Men of few words are the best men." That's from Shakespeare. Samuel Johnson said that, "Language is a dress of thought." Dionysius the Elder said, "Let thy speech be better than silence, or be silent." I hope the listener finds this work to be better than silence.

A wise Spanish proverb goes, "Since we cannot get what we like, let us like what we get." So, you're being exposed to a lot of proverbs. Well, Shakespeare mentioned something that could be useful to you: "Patch grief with proverbs." If you're grieving, listen to some of these quotes and hopefully it'll cheer you up. Emerson said, "The true test of civilization is not the census, not the size of cities, nor of the crops, but the kind of man that the country turns out." "The end of a dissolute life is most commonly a desperate death." Bion said that, and I think that applies to countries as well as people. "In my mind, the best investment the young man starting out in business could possibly make is to give all his time, all his energies, to work, just plain hard work." C.M. Swab said that. It may be going a bit far, but if you don't put enough work into your work, your work won't go very well, that's for sure." Winston Churchill said, "It is a socialist idea that making profits is a vice; I consider the real vice is making losses."

"Brevity is a soul of wit." Shakespeare said that. I hope you find this work to be brief enough.

Emerson said, "Hitch your wagon to a star." Again, that sounds very good, but one can't quite be sure what he meant by that. In those days, for example, they didn't have movie stars. I'm sure he didn't mean that. Some do rise by clinging to the coat tails of others

I'm going to quote something now that I don't agree with, and that's by George Elliot. He says, "Nothing is so good as it seems beforehand," and I think there you can run into the risk of being too cynical. In other words, he might be sounding very philosophical, but it might be that he was disappointed in his marriage or he had a bad picnic or his business didn't turn out or he ordered some product by mail that wasn't as good as he thought and it could be and he may have over-generalized. I think there are some things that are better than they seem or that they appeared beforehand. For example, well, a take a computer that you can use for more things than you thought you could when you got it originally. So I would disagree with that. I think this is an example of something that's wrong when George Elliot said, "Nothing is so good as it seems beforehand." But disappointment is a fact of life. There are projects I've gotten into and investments I've made that have turned sour. There are definitely some things that appear better before hand than in retrospect.

"The winds and waves are always on the side of the ablest navigators." Edward Gibbin said that. "A brain is known by its fruits." H. G. Wells said that. So, you know my brain a little bit because you're seeing some of the fruits.

"The greater the difficulty, the more glory in surmounting it." "Skilled pilots gain their reputations from storms and tempests." Shakespeare said, "There's small choice in rotten apples." Greville said, "It is not enough that you form and even follow the most excellent rules for conducting yourself in the world; you must also know when to deviate from them and where lies the exception." That's very true. That's one of the problems with rigid moral codes. There are times when one must deviate and one must do what one must do to accomplish one's ends. Ernest Hemingway said that, "Courage is grace under pressure." Euripides said, "Cowards do not count in battle. They are there, but not in it."

Theodore Roosevelt said, "No man is worth his salt who is not ready at all times to risk his body, to risk his wellbeing, to risk his life in the great cause." Shakespeare, on the other hand, said that, "The bitter part of valor is discretion."

"Animals are agreeable friends. They ask no questions; they pass no criticisms." I think that's one reason why so many people have pets.

Oliver Wendell Holmes said, "Man has his will but woman has her way," and truer words were never spoken.

"I will find a way, or I will make one." That's by Sir P. Sydney. Sometimes it's necessary to find your own way, as a path is not always available for you to follow.

"The truest wisdom in a general is a resolute determination," and that's from Napoleon. I'd like to comment on that. Since one of my hobbies is playing war games, I don't particularly agree with that. I think that to win warfare, you have to basically outsmart the enemy. Once in a while, courage is necessary, particularly for soldiers. But for general, you don't win just by having courage, or as Napoleon puts, a "resolute determination." You are basically wise by outfoxing the enemy. And I think that's one reason why Napoleon was finally beaten. He thought he could win just by resolute determination. You can't. I mean, people can charge in the mouth of cannons and just be wiped out and kill to a man. And all their determination will mean is that they're going die sooner. But this is not to say that I do not admire those who have great determination. Determination when coupled with good judgment it is the most admirable of virtues. Make a distinction between determination and stubbornness. Determination is continuing with the right thing in spite of obstacles. Stubbornness is doing the wrong thing in spite of punishment. Ruskin said, "Doing is the great thing, for if resolutely people do what is right, in time they will like doing it."

"Do not, then, be afraid of defeat. You are never so near to victory as when defeated in a good cause." That's H.W. Beecher. I feel he is exaggerating there. A major defeat is a horrible thing to endure. If you look at history, you'll find frequently that conquered nations were destroyed and their citizens were reduced to slaves. Frequently, the leaders of the conquered nations would be killed, the wealth of the country would be stolen, and defeat is a very ignominious thing. And frequently in warfare, the defeated do not survive. And it is not just in war where defeat has bad consequences. For example, in business, if your company is defeated by the competition, that may mean bankruptcy for you and the firing of your employees and could well mean the loss of all the time and effort you've invested in your business. So, defeat in business can be quite serious. Defeat say to lose status in the eyes of a woman you love could also be somewhat devastating. I think that people can pull themselves up out of defeat, but I would not say that defeat is very near to victory. It's sort of on the opposite side of the circle, as it were. On the other hand what Beecher said has a lot of merit. If you invest your bound to make some bad investments and lose money. You may well face rejection in your love affairs. Obviously if you play games such as chess, Go, or wargames then you are bound to lose some. If you wrestle with people you're bound to find stronger, faster and more skilled opponents. One definitely should not be paralyzed into inaction due to fear of failure. Not trying is frequently worse than losing.

"Culture is to know the best that has been said and thought in the world," and that's by Matthew Arnold. I hope after reading Great Quotes, you feel that you're a little more cultured. Herbert Samuel said, "A mixture of misery and education is highly explosive." It's interesting that we in the

United States feel that we can better the lives of people in third world countries by quote, unquote, educating them. And I think that's one reason why they have so many revolutions in these countries, and that is that they have a lot of educated people who cannot find good jobs, jobs that are suitable to their education. And perhaps there would be less, shall we say, revolution in these countries if the people were not so well educated. This is especially true if the education is socialist and had politically correct. I'm not saying that most of them are that well educated, but that just educating a few of the young men for jobs that they're not going to get is not going to help the country.

Carlisle said the obvious: "There are but two ways of paying a debt: increase of industry and raising income, or increase of thrift in laying out." In other words, either spend less or make more. Neither is that easy. He neglected the alternative of backruptcy. Viscount Morley said, "In my creed, waste of public money is like a sin against the Holy Ghost." We are a nation of sinners. Our social welfare spending is a sin against the Holy Ghost using Morley's vocabulary.

Socrates said, "Those who want fewest things are nearest to the gods." I think here that Socrates is wrong and that it is not good to want few things. That is one reason why people are poor. If you don't want much, you're not going to work hard and you're not going to get very much. Your desires are, in fact, motivating forces or a motivating force. The more you want, the more you'll do. And the more you do, the more you'll get. So you can realize your desires. Our aspirations are our possibilities. I think that's one reason why the Indians, for example, in India are so poor. They think, okay, I don't want anything. I'll just live a life of complete poverty and that is, per se, saintly. So they end up being extremely poor and deluding themselves into thinking that in some way, they are holy by being poor and not really wanting things and not going out and getting what they want.   But it is wise to avoid clutter and not want items that create an unneeded burden or excess expense. As I said in the book *Do It Right* To have what you want to what it takes. To do what it takes know what it takes. What to do spelled out in the Book *Do Tt Right*

Daniel Webster said, "Employment gives health, sobriety, and morals. Constant employment and well-paid labor produce in a country like ours general prosperity, content, and cheerfulness." I think that is very true. That's one reason why there are revolutions in countries is because of mass unemployment. In fact, that is one of the major campaign platforms that many politicians run on – jobs, jobs, jobs. The idea that one political party or another can provide more employment, or better employment, is a big attraction to the voters. And certainly, unemployment is devastating because a job is for most people their source of income. And without income, you cannot, basically, live well. And not only that, but for many people, a job is a source of satisfaction and self-esteem as well as a way of producing things that are useful for society. And also, it looks very bad on one's resume to say one was unemployed for long periods of time. And so, employment is very important and I think Daniel Webster was right about this. Hilton said, "If you want enemies, excel others; if friends, let others excel you." I think this is another fallacy, and many people believe that if they do well, that people won't like them. Well, it may be that you may not have thousands of friends, or it might be, even, that if you try to conform to the crowd more and don't put out very much that you'll be a little more popular, but you certainly won't get enemies by doing better work. And I think you in the long run will profit by trying to excel other people because you'll feel good about yourself. You'll feel good about yourself if you do the best you can whenever you have the chance, and don't worry about your popularity. If you are popular, you're popular. And if you're not, you're not. And just live with that. But modesty is definitely a virtue. One definitely should not say I am better than you, I work harder, and more creative blah, blah blah. People may not dislike someone who is in some way better than they are but bragging about it is not prudent.

Samuel Johnson said, on the other hand -- and this is a more true statement -- "No man was ever great by imitation," and I agree with that.

You should try to be unique. Try to be yourself. To use hippie jargon, do your own thing. Clark said, "The most terrible of lies is not that which is uttered but that which is lived." And so you don't want to live a lie. You want to be yourself and be proud of it.

Virgil said, "For they conquer who believe they can." And I think this is a fallacy, again, having played war games. I mean, there are countries and there are military situations wherein one country cannot militarily defeat another, and to attempt that would be madness. For example, Hitler, when he invaded Russia. The Russian army was too large and Russia was too vast and the Germans had too many enemies at the time to have seriously considered beating Russia. And yet Hitler invaded and he lost. Although he had very firm belief that he could defeat the Russians. And so, I think that this is a mistake to believe that you can conquer just because you believe you can conquer. You have to have more proof than that. You have to look at the facts and the figures and the numbers and look at the quality of your people as distinct to that of the enemy. But this is not to say that one should not have a very strong self-image is merited. Perhaps one cannot conquer just because one thinks one can but one is surely defeated he believes he cannot conquer. To put it another way to believe one can conquer is necessary but not sufficient.

"No man loves the man whom he fears." Aristotle said that, and I believe that's true. And I think that's one of the fallacies in using harsh discipline on people because then they are not going to like you, and if they don't like you, then they won't work for you. And when the chips are down, when push comes to shove, these people are not going to be on your side. And so you don't want to have people fear you. You want to have people like you. Love might be a little bit strong, but at least they should like you. Shakespeare said, "Uneasy is the head that wears a crown," and I think that is very true. As a student of history, I've noticed that frequently the reason that someone becomes a monarch or a king is because they launch a palace revolution. They murder the old king and seize power violently. And so, being a king, being a monarch, is dangerous. And many a monarch has died due to assassination from someone who was jealous of his power and who wanted to rule in his place. In fact, along the same lines, Sophocles said that, "Fortune is not on the side of the faint hearted," and it takes some courage to rise in the world. It may not be the wise thing to do always, but it takes a lot of courage to attempt to overthrow a monarch, and they who rule were courageous in the sense that they would strike down those who ruled over them. MacBeth is an example in Shakespeare. And there is dangers to that because the followers of the old leader may well rebel against your rule, or it may be that the old leader has enough guards and police and soldiers on his side that your attempt to dispose of him will fail and not only might you die, but it might be that you might die by torture because leaders have that power. Another factor to consider is that attempts to seize power can plunge the country into civil war. As Lincoln said a house divided against itself cannot stand.

"What you dislike in another, take care to correct in yourselves" - Spratt. "Reprove thy friend privately. Mend him publicly." Solomon said that. I think that's also good advice for a supervisor. Employees do not like to be publicly criticized, but they do like public praise. So that is a good piece of advice for a supervisor. "Doing easily what others find difficult is talent. Doing what is impossible for talent is genius." Wendell Phillips is quoted as saying, "One on God's side is majority?" Alexander Hamilton gave another quote on genius: "Men give me credit for some genius. All the genius I have lies in this: When I have a subject in hand, I study it profoundly; day and night, it is before me. My mind becomes pervaded with and the effort which I have made is what people are pleased to call the fruit of genius. This is the fruit of labor and thought." "The greater the power, the more dangerous the abuse. " Edmond Burke said that. I think that's one of the dangers in communism where the government controls everything. There is always the danger for great abuses of power there. And another quote on government: "What is the best government? That which teaches us to govern ourselves." I think the same thing applies to being a good supervisor. A good supervisor would have his employees do themselves the work that is needed without prodding from him. The law is made to protect the innocent by punishing the guilty. Shakespeare said, "They laugh that win."

Goethe along the same lines said, "Men show their character in nothing more clearly than what they think laughable." William Ernest Henley said, "I am the master of my fate. The captain of my soul." To be successful one must be accountable. One must not blame others for one's misfortune but rather take responsibility for one's fate. Howel said, "He who has no inclination to learn more will be very apt to think that he knows enough already." But can never learn too much. Thinking one knows all there is about a subject is a barrier to further knowledge. Why would do some people stop learning as soon as they graduate from school? That's a major mistake. You can never know too much, and to assume you have all the knowledge you need is to say that you are going to stay ignorant for the rest of your life. Euripides said, "He who neglects learning in his youth loses the past and is dead for the future." People never give up their liberties but under some delusion," and that's from Burke. Jefferson said, "Eternal vigilance is the price of liberty." I think we see in many countries in the world, communism and other forms of leftist dictatorship, and I think the reason for that is the people there are not vigilant and they lost their liberty. Let's not let it happen here. Eternal vigilance is, indeed, the price of liberty. Patrick Henry said, "I know not what course others may take. But as for me, give me liberty or give me death." And those are inspired words by a great man.

Tenyson said, "Tis better to have loved and lost than to never have loved at all." And I think that's very profound, very true. Shakespeare said, "The course of true love never was smooth." And I think that's true for more than love and also for life in general. You've got to expect ups and downs. I'm sure you can say the same thing about a business. The course of a business never did run totally smoothly. The course of a military campaign does run totally smoothly. A manufacturing project does not always run totally smoothly. There are always problems, and it's up to you as a competent individual to overcome these problems. Literature is the immortality of speech. That's from Schlegel. Virgil is quoted as saying, "It never troubles the wolf how the sheep may be." "Man in the right with God on his side is in the majority, though he be alone." That's from H. W. Beecher. Shakespeare said, "Lord, what fools these mortals be?" Shakespeare again, "He was a man, take him, for all in all I shall not look upon his life again." I think that's a valid point that there are unique individuals in history who had great impact. For example, Scipio Africanus, in Roman history, Alexander the Great, Charles Darwin in science, and Henry Ford in manufacturing . There are other people who have made tremendous contributions in warfare or science or the arts and so on. There are a lot of people that made significant contributions and who are unique.

Montague said, "There is no man so good who, were he to submit all his thoughts and actions to the law, would not deserve hanging ten times in his life, maybe more." It's a good thing you're judged by your actions and not by your thoughts, right? Schiller said, "The voice of the majority is no proof of justice. It's no proof of anything else, either." Shakespeare said, "Men at some time are masters of their fates." I hope you're learning from these maxims. Sir J. Mackintosh said, "Maxims are the condensed good sense of nations." So what you're getting now is the condensed good sense of nations, and I hope you appreciate that. Richard Rumbold said, "I never could believe that providence had sent a few men into the world ready booted and spurred to ride, and millions ready saddled and bridled to be ridden." That's the way history appears or appears to be, only a few people who are capable of leading and great multitudes who are merely led. But that's life. It's very strange, but that's the way things are. Washington Irving said, "Little minds are tamed and subdued by misfortune, but great minds rise above it." And I think that is an excellent point. Everybody has some things that happen in their life that they don't like. But if you had everything happen that you wanted to happen, then you would just want more. So it's bound to be that way. I mean, you can't have everything because the more you get, the more you're going to want. So don't be subdued or tamed by misfortune, but rise above your misfortunes and keep trying. Cicero said, "Any man may make a mistake, but none but a fool will continue in it." Unfortunately, there are a lot of fools in the world.

Gladstone said along the same line, "No man ever became great or good except through many and great mistakes." I think that's a valid point. You have to try things. Sure, sometimes you'll fall down. Sure, sometimes your business deals won't go through. Sure, sometimes your sales won't be as good as you like. You have to keep trying. Remember that you can't be great except through mistakes. You have to learn what works and what doesn't.

Johnson said, "The art of memory is the art of attention." And you should pay attention to small details. Quote Shakespeare again: "Memory, the warder of the brain." Cicero: "Taxes are the sinews of the state." And I think that's the valid point that government needs tax revenues in order to survive, just like a business needs income. The government also needs income. And the government gets its income through taxes, so taxes are necessary. This is not to say that in many countries taxes are not too high, and that in many countries there's a lot of waste in government. But that is not to say that the government doesn't need taxes. And Cicero says, "They are the sinews of the state."

Goethe said, "Nature is a living visible garment of God." Therefore, it is wise to study nature, I think, because you're studying the works of God. The creator and the created by one. One more biblical quote is they have sown the wind and reaped the whirlwind.

The Bible says the wages of sin is death. It says further that the fashions of this world passes away. Another quote is if God is with us who can be against us? One of the most moving biblical quotes is the Truth shall make you free. The Bible also says great is truth and mighty above all things.

"You should hammer your iron while it is glowing hot." That's from Cyrus. Publilious Cyrus. That's a valid point. You have to seize opportunities while they're there, while you have them in hand. You may never get another chance. And Disraeli said, "Next to knowing when to seize opportunity, the most important thing in life is to know when to forgo an advantage." It's possible that you may make a mistake by pursuing an opportunity where you really shouldn't. Or there really isn't an opportunity, but it appears to be an opportunity.

Shakespeare said, "He jests at scars that never felt a wound." Shakespear again: "How poor are they that have not patience?" That's very true. Another little cliché: "Rome was not built in a day." And you have to have patience and you have to take the time to do a good job at what you're doing. Shakespeare: "In many strokes though , you down and fell the hardest timbered oak." Another saying on patience: "Patience is bitter, but its fruit is sweet." And that's from Rousseau. I'll now quote the New Testament: "Knock and the door will open to you, where it is always the one who asks who receives. The one who searches who finds and the one who knocks to whom the door opens." That's a valid point there. You have to try, and if you don't try, you'll never succeed. "Treason doth never prosper, for if it prosper, none dare call it treason." I think that's another very valid point. Frequently there are shifts in political nations of leaders of the countries. And when the political philosophy of a leader's change, they may well imprison supporters of the old regime. So what may have been treason to an old administration has suddenly become established policy, and those who hold to the old views are, shall we say, eliminated, so that's why treason doth never prosper, because when it does prosper, it's not considered treason anymore. Very funny.

Shakespeare again: "Some rise by sin and some by virtue fall." I certainly hope that I never fall by virtue. But that is not to imply that I want to rise by sin. On the other hand, "I would rather shun the bait than struggle in the snare." That's a little modification of Dryden in this quote. "Better shun the bait than struggle in the snare." I quoted Shakespeare repeatedly, I'll do it again. But I disagree with this later quote. He said there, "There is nothing either good or bad, but thinking makes it so." That's a philosophical idea that I don't agree with. I think there are absolute goods and bads. It's not just a matter of what you think about it, but what it actually is. There are some things that are decidedly bad such as destroying the environment. And that's not just a matter of your thinking about it or saying that it's good or bad, it actually is good or bad in the absolute sense. So I disagree with Shakespeare when he says, "There is nothing good or bad, but thinking makings it so." Ford said, "Thinking is the hardest work there is, which is the probable reason why so few engage in it." It must be true because few people do engage in it. I don't really think that it is hard work. Engaging in considerable thought myself I say that. The Great Longfellow said, "Sit and revere and watch the changing color of the waves that break on the idle seashore of the mind." I take it that's what you as a reader are doing, watching the colorful waves that break on the idle seashore of the mind. "Some persons do first, think afterward, and then repent forever." Yeah, I must admit that there are things in my life that I repent doing. I acted reflexively at times when it was imprudent to do so. But on the other hand one should not be paralyzed into inaction by fear of failure.

Coolridge said, "Picture is an intermediate something between a thought and a word." This brings to mind an excellent point, and that's that it's very good to draw, to picture your ideas visually using drawing as a graphic means of expressing yourself. It's why it's good to have, oh, say, paper and pencil to hand or have chalkboard when you want to communicate to other people, because of the importance of visualization and thought. It's why drafting is so important. It's why architects design plans, and so on. The plan is sort of the intermediate between a thought and the thing itself. "Thinking," according to Plato, "is the talking of the soul with itself." "Thought is the property of those only who can entertain it." Franklin said, "Dost thou love live? Then do not squander time, for that is the stuff life is made of." That's a very valid point. You don't want to waste time because it is the most precious resource. Franklin on time again, "Never put off till tomorrow that which you can do today." Plutarch said, "The whole life of man is it but a point of time. Let's enjoy it, therefore, while it lasts and not spend it to no purpose. Tennyson said, "Never mourning wore till evening, but some heart did break." Well, I say just as long as it isn't my heart, that's okay.

"Trifles make perfection, but perfection itself is no trifle." And that's from Michelangelo. He should know, being a great artist. Along the same lines from Ecclesiasticus, "He that despises small things shall fail by little and little." I certainly hope I don't fail let alone little by little. H. W. Beecher: "Troubles are often the tools by which God fashions us for better things. Sophocles said, "The truth is always the strongest argument. " For that I say, I wish it were true. I just wish it were true. I really believe you can tell the truth over and over to some people and they'll never believe it. It'll never sink in. Dryden said, "Truth is a foundation of all knowledge and the cement of all societies." Emerson said, "The years teach much which the days will never know." And that's one reason why I think in many countries, the old are given respect because they've learned a lot through long experience. Not all people learn and not all old people are wise, but I think if somebody is diligently seeking knowledge that the older he gets the more he'll know and the more valuable his opinion is. You learn as you age if you try to do that.

"He is truly wise who gains wisdom from others' mishaps." And that's a valid point. You should not repeat the mistakes of others. If you're going to make a mistake, try to make an original mistake rather than following the errors of others. Syrus said, "He is truly wise who gains wisdom from another's mishap." Well, it's certainly a lot easier to gain knowledge from another's mishap than from your own. You want to learn from other's errors if you can. Then avoid those errors.

"A child can ask a thousand questions that the wise man cannot answer." Shakespeare said, "A lion among ladies is a most dreadful thing." A woman's liber wouldn't agree with that statement. "For a wife take the daughter of a good woman." And that's from Fuller. I think that's kind of hard to do nowadays because you may not even know the mother of your wife or your future wife.

"God gives every bird its food, but he does not throw it into the nest." That's from J. G. Holland. Tennyson said, "So many worlds, so much to do, so little done. Such things to be." Beechmore is quoted as saying, "It is a sober truth that people who live only to amuse themselves work harder at the task than most people do in earning their daily bread." That's true. A lot of people spend more energy in their hobbies than they do in their work. Well, their work is supporting them and their hobbies are a diversion. A pleasant diversion, but a diversion. Sir James Matthew Berrie, "Nothing is really work unless you would rather be doing something else." So true. So true. "Life is the task and many share the toil," and that's from Homer. That's a bit too grim. Johnson is quoted as saying, "The two most engaging powers of an author are to make new things familiar and familiar things new." I hope I've done that at least a little bit of that.

Goethe said, "Girls we love for what they are, young men for what they promise to be." "Cooperation is doing with a smile what you have to do anyway." And that comes from *Quote Magazine*. Golda Meir is very witty in her comment of, "Don't be so humble. You're not that great." General Features Corporation, if you can imagine a corporation being quoted, says, "Plan ahead. It wasn't raining when Noah built the ark."

The noted Theodore White writes, "The American dream is not over. America is an adventure." How true, how true. William Seron says, "Kids are always the only future the human race has." And I say, the human race is in trouble. We are forgetting racial equality and eugenics to our peril. The Third World countries of nonwhite people's have a much higher birthrate than white Europeans and Americans. And they are coming to Europe and America in large numbers.

Of course we couldn't get by without quoting "Dizzy" Dean saying, "It ain't bragging if you really done it." General George S. Patton says, "Take calculated risks." That's quite different from being rash.

Remember that. Leo Burnett says, "When you reach for the stars, you may not quite get one, but you wouldn't come up with a handful of mud, either." Nelson Mandela is a leading communist in South Africa and he works for the African National Congress, which is a communist front organization, and I'd like to quote him: "We communist party members are the most advanced revolutionaries in modern history. The enemy must be completely crushed and wiped out from the face of the earth before a communist world can be realized." Again, that's from Nelson Mandela of the African National Congress.

Another quote from the, quote, unquote, illustrious Nelson Mandela, "The cause of communism is the greatest cause in the history of mankind because it seeks to remove from society all forms of oppression and exploitation, to liberate mankind, and to ensure peace and prosperity to all." I think this illustrates the idea that is very dangerous, and that's misguided idealism and it's all too common. Here you see an arch communist and a professional revolutionary who's sprouting idealistic phrases, and yet his actions are highly dangerous to civilization.

The great author George Orwell says, "Who controls the present controls the past; who controls the past controls the future." That brings to mind interesting point that you should be concerned about the authenticity of information you receive about the past. There are those who would distort information about the past to manipulate present thinking. "He who controls the past controls the future." Another quote from Nietzsche: "What in the world has caused more damage than the follies of the compassionate?" Another comment from Nietzsche: "To the children, I am still a learned man," he writes, "I am pushed out from the house of the learned and have slammed the door behind me." There is a lot of truth to Nietzsche saying. His philosophy is not consistent. And I think there are many mistakes in what he says. I think he is interesting to listen to and, in fact, should not be considered so much a philosopher as a poet. And I would define a poet as someone who says things that may not be true but sound good. And the poet is concerned about how things sound rather than the truth behind what is said. And Nietzsche would be classified, in spite of what some may say, as a poet. A master poet. One of the best poets that ever lived. This isn't to say that you can't find some wisdom in what he says, and I quoted aspects of Nietzsche which I feel are valid. This is not to say that everything he says or even that most of what Nietzsche says is correct. There's a way of poetic nonsense in Nietzsche, but there are some good points such as the ones quoted

Robert Conquest once observed, "It can hardly be called progress, and I would add openness or reform when cannibals learn to use utensils like forks and knives." Hadley said, "Life is not a goblet to be trained. It is a measure to be filled."

Napoleon Hill said, "If you do not believe in cooperation, look what happens to a wagon that loses a wheel." Napoleon Hill again: "Don't be afraid of a little opposition. Remember that the kite of success generally rises against the wind of adversity, not with it." Another comment from Napoleon Hill: "Never in the history of the world has there been such abundant opportunity as there is now for the person who is willing to serve before trying to collect." Another comment from Napoleon Hill: "The only lasting favor which the parent may confer upon the child is that of helping the child to help himself." All salesmen will do well to remember that no one wants anything that someone else is trying to get rid of. Another quote from Napoleon Hill. "When you do not know what to do or which way to turn, smile. This will relax your mind and let the sunshine of happiness into your soul." "Cherish your visions and your dreams, as they are the children of your soul; the blueprints of your ultimate achievements," again, from Napoleon Hill. Further from Napoleon Hill: "No good thinker will judge another person by that which the other person's enemies say about him." "The man who accurately knows just what we wants in life has already gone a long way toward attaining it." Employers are always on the lookout for a man who does a better job of any sort than is customary, whether it be wrapping a package, writing a letter, or closing a sale. These quotes are from Napoleon Hill.

From the Sanskrit: "Yesterday is but a dream; tomorrow is only a vision. But today, well-lived makes every yesterday a dream of happiness and every tomorrow a vision of hope. Look well, therefore, to this day." Again, from the Sanskrit.

The great Ralph Waldo Emerson said: "There is no defeat except from within. There is really no insurmountable barrier save your own inherent weakness of purpose." I think he's exaggerating a little bit, but I think there is a lot of truth to that and we certainly don't want to be defeated too easily from within, you don't want to give up too quickly, and you don't want to be weak of purpose. Another quote from Napoleon Hill: "In every soul there has been the deposited seed of a great future, but that seed will never germinate, much less grow to maturity, except through the rendering of useful service." From Napoleon Hill again: "A man is half lost the moment he begins to feel sorry for himself or spin an alibi with which he would explain away his defects." Final quote from Napoleon Hill: "Time is a master worker that heels the wounds of temporary defeat, equalizes the inequalities and rights, the wrongs of the world. There is nothing impossible with time." Again, I think Napoleon Hill is exaggerating a bit. If you study physics, you will realize there are certain things that cannot be done physically. The laws of physics do provide limitations to what can be done. No object can be made to travel faster than the speed of light, for example. There are certain, what is referred to conservation laws in physics, for example, matter or energy is conserved. And there are other laws of physics that men cannot disobey, as it were. The laws of nature prevent these physical laws from being violated. But aside from the laws of physics, I think that we can greatly expand one's capabilities, and we can do incredible things. I'm sure if you look at the world in a few hundred years from now, you'll find that man's progress has been incredible and that technological advance is always possible to the most incredible degree. Things that are impossible today will be possible tomorrow. This is not to say that anything can be done, but it is to say that incredibly advanced things can be done that are not dreamed of today.

Conclusion

John Wilson said, "Oh for a book and a shady nook either indoor or out." I hope the reader finds that shady nook while reading *Great Quotes* or *Do It Right* or Jokes? Or *Consulting for Profit* Which are my other books to date.

Shakespeare said, "The saying is true, The empty vessel makes the greatest sound." I trust that I was not just making empty sounds when writing *Great Quotes*. Another quote from the great author, "Patch griefs with proverbs." This was my intent.

Ruggiero Leoncavallo said, "The comedy is finished" I would add there is truth humor.

So to conclude *Great Quotes* This phrase from Shakespeare, *"The rest is silence."*